Read and Remember

Individual and Group Activities
for Fiction and Nonfiction Reading

AUTHORS

Mandy Lohman

and

Erin Richardson

Carson-Dellosa Publishing Company, Inc.
Greensboro, North Carolina

DEDICATION

This series is dedicated to Chris Lohman and Kevin Richardson for their continued support and encouragement throughout this project.

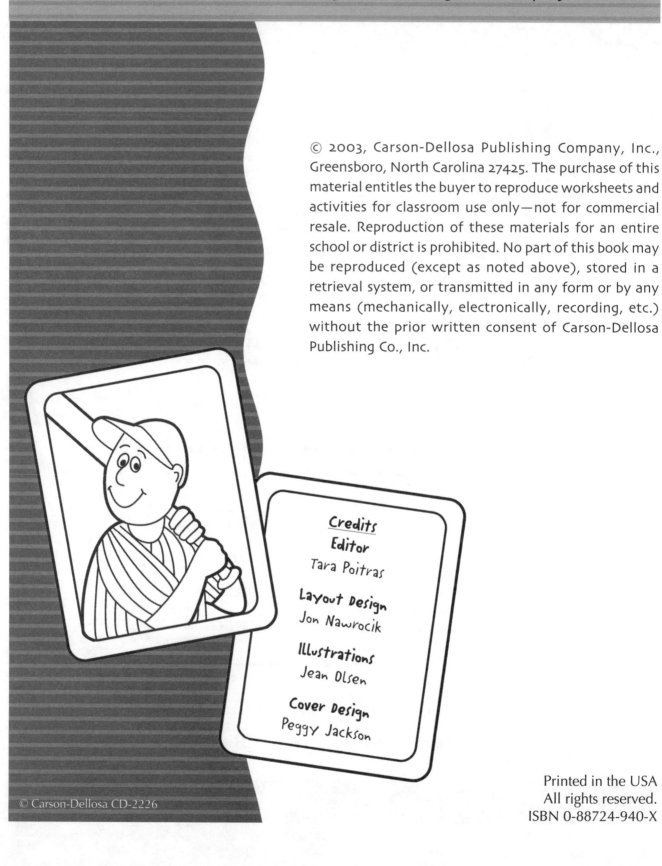

Credits

Editor
Tara Poitras

Layout Design
Jon Nawrocik

Illustrations
Jean Olsen

Cover Design
Peggy Jackson

Table of Contents

Introduction

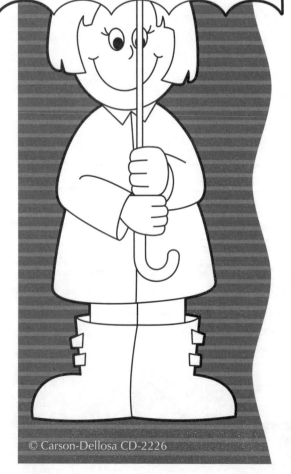

Help students read **and** remember! The creative activities in this book were designed to improve students' reading comprehension skills—by addressing one story element at a time.

To help students focus on each story detail, activities are divided into four sections: Character, Setting, Plot, and Overall Story.

Activities for both fiction and nonfiction selections are included in each section. The activities can be completed by individual students, with partners, or by small groups. A quick visual reference is included at the bottom of each page to help teachers and students choose an appropriate activity. See the examples to the left.

Teachers can make packets of various activities for each student. Or, the activities can be used in a reading center, where students choose an activity to complete after they have read a fiction or nonfiction selection. During reading-group time, teachers can work with a small group of students to complete an activity. Advanced students that need to be challenged with independent work will also benefit from completing these activities.

Activity instructions ("What You Do") address the student. They can be photocopied for students to read themselves, or the teacher can give verbal instructions. A materials list ("What You Need") is included for each activity. Items are listed in the order students will use them. Some activities also include "Supplies You Could Use," a list of additional materials students might use to complete an activity.

Most activities include a "Note to the Teacher." This section includes any specific directions for the teacher, plus options for completing the activity.

Master List of Materials

What You Need:
brad (1)
card stock (optional)
ceramic tile (white, 8" x 8")
clothes hangers (2)
colored pencils
construction paper (assorted colors, including brown)
craft stick
crayons
drawing paper
envelope
gift tag
glue
greeting cards (old)
hole punch
looseleaf book rings (2)
magazines (optional)
markers
paint (for ceramic tiles)
paintbrush
paint shirt or smock
paper lunch bag
pencil
permanent markers
poster board
scissors
shoe box
sock
stapler
tagboard (optional)
tape
tissue or wrapping paper
twist ties or rubber bands (optional)
white paper
writing paper
yarn or string

Supplies You Could Use:
beads
buttons
colored paper
crayon shavings
fabric
fabric crayons
felt
glitter
hot glue
leaves
pasta
pencil shavings
rice
sand
sandpaper
sequins
wood chips

Delicious Grapes

What You Do:

1. Create a delicious picture of grapes to describe a character from a book you have read.

2. On the Delicious Grapes Template, lightly color the stem brown and the leaves green.

3. Write the book title on one leaf and the author's name on the other leaf.

4. Write the character's name on the stem.

5. Lightly color the grapes purple. Then, write an adjective about the character on each grape.

6. Cut out the grapes, leaves, and stem.

7. Glue the stem and the leaves to a sheet of construction paper.

8. Glue the grapes to the picture, in the form of a bunch. Glue three grapes on the top, two underneath, and one on the bottom.

9. Write your name on the back of the picture.

Notes to the Teacher:

- If desired, students can complete a picture of grapes for each character in the book.

- Remind students to color lightly so that they can easily write on the stem, leaves, and grapes after coloring them.

What You Need:

Delicious Grapes Template

colored pencils

pencil

scissors

glue

9" x 12" construction paper

Delicious Grapes Template

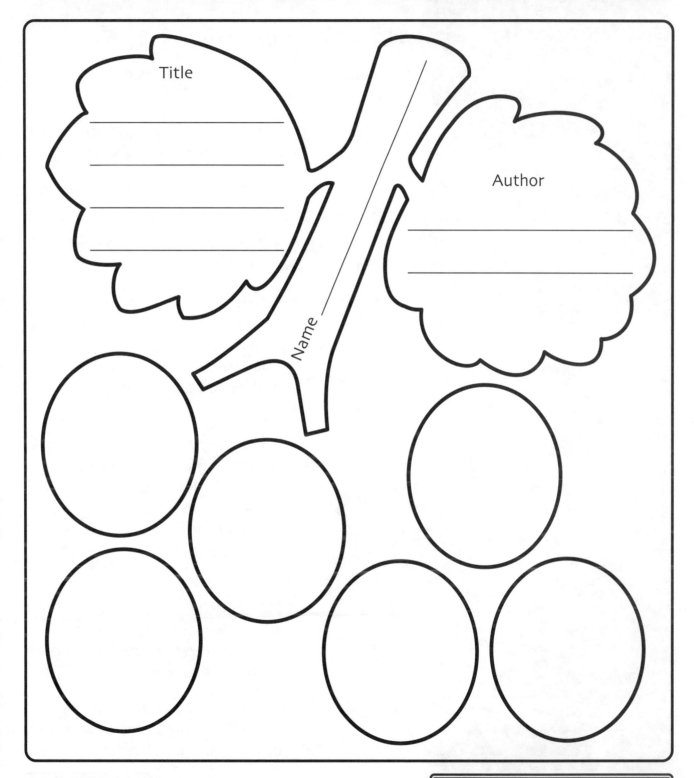

Title

Author

Name

Wanted Poster

What You Do:

1. Make a wanted poster for a character in a book you have read.

2. Draw and color a picture of the character in the box on the Wanted Poster Activity Sheet.

3. Write the character's name on the line labeled "Who."

4. What does the character look like? Describe him in the section labeled "Description."

5. In the section labeled "Wanted for," write one to three sentences to explain why the character is wanted. Use events from the book and your imagination to help you create and write your explanation.

   For example, the wolf in *Little Red Riding Hood* could be wanted for chasing Grandma into the closet. He lied to Little Red Riding Hood by pretending he was her grandmother. He also scared Little Red Riding Hood with his big teeth.

6. How much money would you give someone if she "captured" the character? Write a reward amount on the line labeled "Reward."

7. Write the book title, author's name, and your name on the back of the wanted poster.

What You need:

Wanted Poster
Activity Sheet

markers, crayons,
colored pencils

pencil

Wanted Poster Activity Sheet

WANTED

Who _____

Description _____

_____

Wanted for _____

_____

_____

$ Reward _____

Character Gift

What You Do:

1. Give a gift to a character from a book you have read.

2. Draw and color a picture of the gift on white paper. Make sure that the gift is appropriate for the character. For example, you might give Little Red Riding Hood a new cape.

3. Complete the information on the Character Gift Activity Sheet.

4. Place the picture and activity sheet in a shoe box and wrap it with tissue or wrapping paper.

5. Write the character's name on a gift tag and tape it to the gift.

Notes to the Teacher:

- If desired, boxes can be covered with blank paper, and students can decorate them with pictures from their books.

- The boxes and lids could be covered separately, so the gifts can be opened without unwrapping them. The wrapping could also be done in advance for the students.

- After the students have made their gifts, they can exchange presents. Each student can unwrap a gift and then read the Character Gift Activity Sheet to the rest of the class.

What You Need:

white paper

pencil

markers, colored pencils, crayons

Character Gift Activity Sheet

shoe box

tissue or wrapping paper

scissors

tape

gift tag

Character Gift Activity Sheet

Your name _____

Title _____

Author _____

Character's name _____

Description of character _____

_____

_____

_____

Name of gift _____

_____

I gave this gift to this character because _____

_____

_____

_____

_____

_____

_____

_____

ABC Poetry Book

What You Do:

1. Create a poetry book about the characters from a book your group has read.

2. Select a character and write her name on the top line of the ABC Poetry Book Template. This will be the title of the poem.

3. Rewrite the character's name on the next line. Then, using the first letter of the name, write the next four letters of the alphabet on the beginning of the next four lines. If you reach the end of the alphabet, start again with "A."

4. Use these letters to write short phrases that describe the character. Here is an example:

   Cinderella
   Danced with the prince
   Evil stepsisters didn't like her
   Fairy godmother made her a dress
   Grateful for her mice friends

5. Color the template. Then, repeat these steps for the other characters in the book.

6. As a group, use construction paper to create a cover for the poetry book. Write the book title, author's name, your name, and the names of the classmates in your group on the cover.

7. Staple the cover and poems together.

Note to the Teacher:
Assign students to small groups to read a book together. Each student should pick one character to write a poem about.

What You need:
ABC Poetry Book Template

pencil

crayons, colored pencils

construction paper

stapler

ABC Poetry Book Template

TRADING CARDS

What You Do:

1. Make trading cards for two characters from a book you have read.

2. Write the book title and author's name on the first card on the Trading Cards Template.

3. Describe the character in the section labeled "Statistics." Write one to three sentences that tell about the character you chose.

4. Draw and color a picture of the character in the box on the left side of the card.

5. Write the character's name above the picture.

6. Write your name under your description of the character.

7. Cut out the card.

8. Fold the trading card on the dashed line and glue or tape the two sides together.

9. Repeat these steps for the second trading card.

Note to the Teacher:
If desired, photocopy the template on card stock for extra durability.

What You need:
Trading Cards Template

pencil

markers, crayons, colored pencils

scissors

glue or tape

Trading Cards Template

CHARACTER

Title _____

Author _____

Statistics _____

_____

_____

_____

_____

_____

_____

_____

Name _____

CHARACTER

Title _____

Author _____

Statistics _____

_____

_____

_____

_____

_____

_____

Name _____

Sock Puppets

What You Do:

1. Stage a puppet show with two or three characters from a book your group has read.

2. Use materials from your classroom's craft box to make sock puppets for the characters your group has selected. Some supplies you could use are listed below.

3. Draw and color a picture of the setting on a piece of poster board.

4. Use the puppets and the poster board setting to act out the story or part of the story with your group.

Supplies You Could Use:

buttons	felt
colored paper	paint
construction paper	sequins
fabric	string
fabric crayons	yarn

Notes to the Teacher:

- Assign two or three students to read a book together.

- Each student should make a puppet for a different character. The students can then act out the story together.

- Students could also write a script, which they can read as they act out the story.

What You Need:

sock

scissors

glue

hot glue (optional)

poster board

pencil

markers, crayons

Storyboard

What You Do:

1. Make a storyboard that shows the setting of a book your group has read.

2. As a group, draw and color a picture of the setting on a piece of poster board.

3. Use scissors to make a horizontal slit in the board, about two inches from the bottom. Leave a two-inch margin on each side of the slit.

4. Select a character from the book. Draw and color a picture of the character on a sheet of construction paper or tagboard. Then, cut out the picture and glue a craft stick to the back.

5. When you and your group have made all of the characters, write a script for them based on the events in the book.

6. Slide the characters through the slit in the storyboard and read the script.

Notes to the Teacher:

• Assign students to small groups to read a book together.

• Each student should make a different character.

• When the students have completed their storyboards, they can present them and read the script to the rest of the class.

• If students have read a chapter book, they can act out a chapter instead of the entire book. They could also make a storyboard for the setting of each chapter.

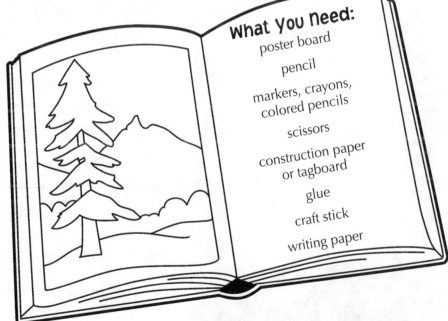

What you need:
poster board
pencil
markers, crayons, colored pencils
scissors
construction paper or tagboard
glue
craft stick
writing paper

Tile Setting

What You Do:

1. Recreate the setting of a book you have read by painting it on a tile.

2. Draw a picture of the setting on drawing paper. This will help you get ready to paint on the tile.

3. When you have completed the drawing, paint or draw the same picture on the white tile. Be sure to wear a paint shirt or smock.

4. Use a permanent marker to write the book title, author's name, and your name on the back of the tile.

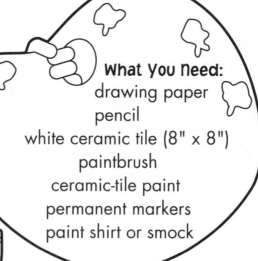

What You Need:
drawing paper
pencil
white ceramic tile (8" x 8")
paintbrush
ceramic-tile paint
permanent markers
paint shirt or smock

Notes to the Teacher:

- Special paint for ceramic tiles can be purchased at a craft store. This paint also comes in pen form, which may be easier for students to use.

- With the help of the art teacher, students could glaze their tiles and then fire them in a kiln.

Texture Setting

What You Do:

1. Make a textured picture of the setting of a book you have read.

2. Draw and color a picture of the setting on a piece of poster board.

3. Add texture to the picture by gluing different items from your classroom's craft box to the poster board. Some supplies you could use are listed below.

4. Write the book title, author's name, and your name on the back of the poster board.

Supplies You Could Use:

beads	glitter	pencil shavings	string
construction paper	leaves	rice	tissue paper
crayon shavings	paint	sand	wood chips
fabric	pasta	sandpaper	yarn

Note to the Teacher:
Heavy or bulky items may adhere better with hot glue than with regular glue.

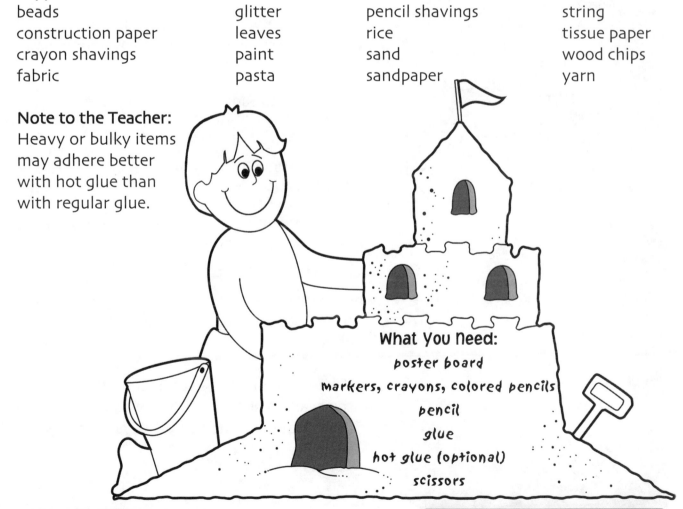

What You Need:
poster board
markers, crayons, colored pencils
pencil
glue
hot glue (optional)
scissors

SETTING MAP

What You Do:

1. Follow the characters of a book your group has read by making a map of different locations.

2. Brainstorm with your group the different places from the book you could include on the map.

3. Use the information your group learned in the book and your imaginations to draw and color a map of the setting using the Setting Map Template.

4. Label the important places on your map. For example, you could draw and label these places from *Little Red Riding Hood*:

   Little Red Riding Hood's house
   Grandma's house
   The forest
   The woodcutter's house
   The wolf's den

5. Write the book title, author's name, your name, and the names of the classmates in your group on the back of your setting map.

Notes to the Teacher:
- Assign students to small groups to read a book together.

- When students have completed their maps, they can present them to the rest of the class. Maps can then be displayed for other students to read.

What You Need:

SETTING MAP
TEMPLATE

PENCIL

MARKERS, CRAYONS,
COLORED PENCILS

X you
are
here

Setting Map Template

STORY STOPLIGHT

What You Do:

1. Create a story stoplight to show how the plot of a book you have read "stops" and "goes."

2. Lightly color the lights on the Story Stoplight Templates. Color one red, one yellow, and one green.

3. On the red light, write about a problem that one or more characters experienced.

4. On the yellow light, write the solution that the character(s) used to solve the problem.

5. On the green light, write how the story ends with that solution.

6. Color the rectangle yellow and write the book title and author's name on it.

7. Cut out the rectangle and three lights.

8. Glue the rectangle to the top of the sheet of construction paper and write your name on the bottom.

9. Glue the lights in order (red, yellow, green) under the rectangle.

Notes to the Teacher:

- Cut sheets of 12" x 18" brown construction paper in half vertically for students to make the stoplights.

- Remind students to color lightly so that they can easily write on the lights and rectangle after coloring them.

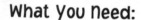

What You Need:

Story Stoplight Templates

colored pencils

pencil

scissors

glue

6" x 18" sheet of brown construction paper

Story Stoplight Template #1

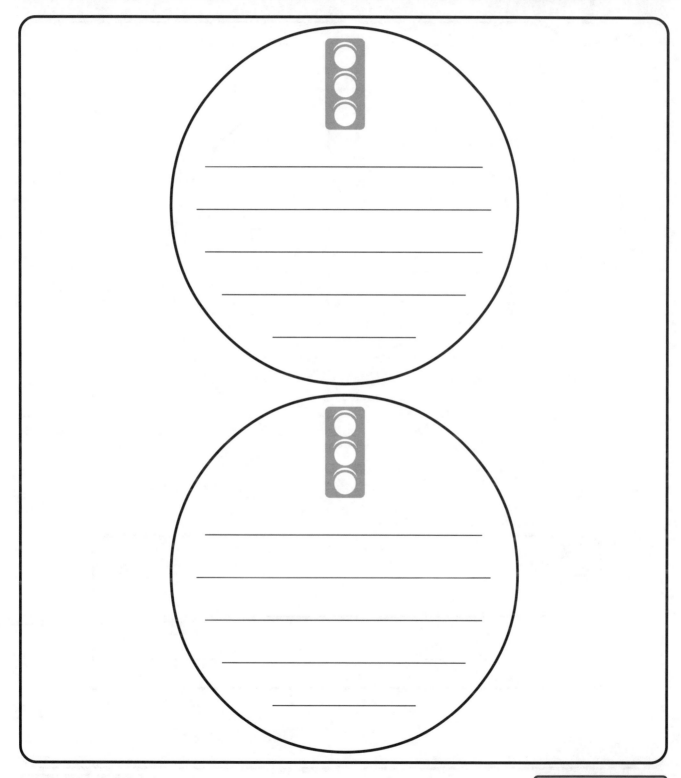

Story Stoplight Template #2

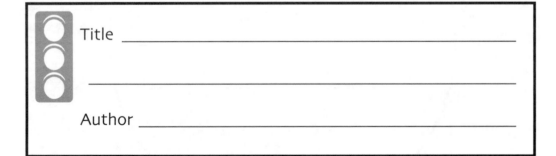

Title _____

_____

Author _____

Greeting Card

What You Do:

1. Send a greeting card to a character from a book you have read.

2. Look at different types of greeting cards to get ideas. Some types of cards are: congratulations, get well, birthday, anniversary, missing you, sympathy, and holiday.

3. Brainstorm ideas for your card. The type of card you choose should be appropriate for the character and the events that occurred in the book. For example, if the character went on a trip, a "missing you" card would be appropriate.

4. Fold a sheet of construction paper or card stock in half to form the card.

5. Write a greeting on the front of the card. Draw and color a picture to match the greeting.

6. On the inside of the card, complete the message. Include in your message three or four details about the events from the book. Then, sign your name.

7. Write the book title and author's name on the back of the card. Write one or two sentences to explain why you chose this type of card.

Notes to the Teacher:

- Bring in a variety of greeting cards to share with the class, and encourage students to bring in old cards from home.

- Students can also make and address envelopes for their cards. The addresses can be the students' own or addresses they have made up.

What You Need:
old greeting cards

construction paper or card stock

pencil

crayons, markers

Paper Bag Clues

What You Do:

1. Challenge a classmate to discover what book you have read by giving him clues about the plot of your book.

2. Collect small items that represent events from the beginning, middle, and end of the book. If you cannot find objects, draw and color a picture of each item on construction paper and cut it out. Or, you can cut out pictures from magazines.

3. Write the name of each object on the top line of the clue cards on the Paper Bag Clues Template.

4. On each clue, describe how the object fits with that part of the book.

5. Cut out the clue cards and place them in an envelope.

6. Decorate a paper lunch bag. Do not include the book title or any other information about the book.

7. Place the envelope and the objects and/or pictures in the bag.

8. Use a marker to write the book title, author's name, and your name on the bottom of the bag.

9. Trade your paper bag with another student's. Use his clues to discover what book he read.

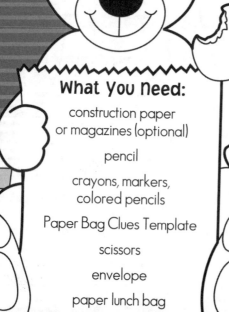

What You need:

construction paper
or magazines (optional)

pencil

crayons, markers,
colored pencils

Paper Bag Clues Template

scissors

envelope

paper lunch bag

Paper Bag Clues Template

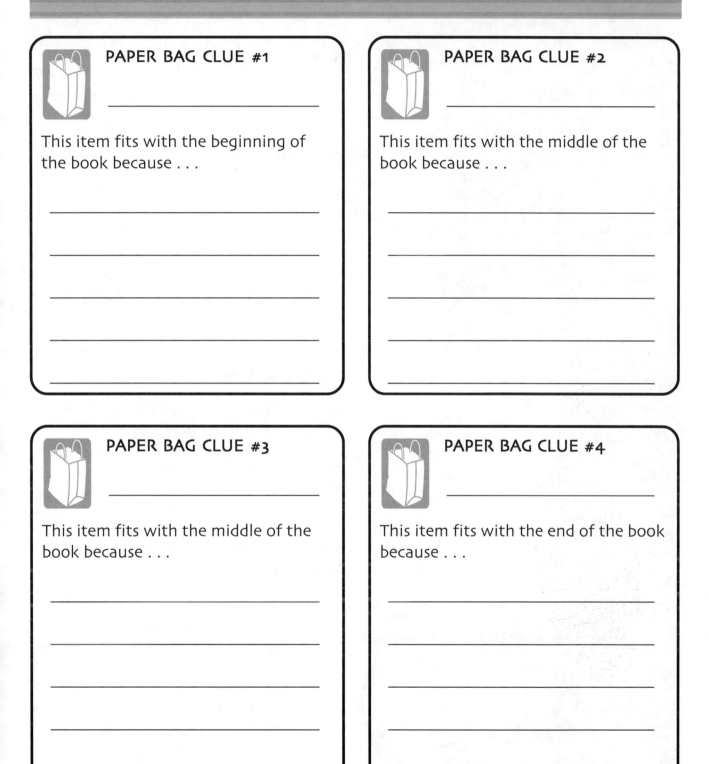

PAPER BAG CLUE #1

_____

This item fits with the beginning of the book because . . .

_____

_____

_____

_____

PAPER BAG CLUE #2

_____

This item fits with the middle of the book because . . .

_____

_____

_____

_____

PAPER BAG CLUE #3

_____

This item fits with the middle of the book because . . .

_____

_____

_____

_____

PAPER BAG CLUE #4

_____

This item fits with the end of the book because . . .

_____

_____

_____

_____

Story Wheel

What You Need:
Story Wheel Templates
pencil
colored pencils, markers
scissors
brad
Story Wheel Activity Sheet

What You Do:

1. Make a story wheel to show the important events from a book you have read.

2. Write the book title and author's name on Story Wheel Template #1.

3. In section 1, draw and color a picture of an event from the beginning of the book. In section 2, draw and color a picture of an event from the middle of the book. In section 3, draw and color a picture of an event from the end of the book.

4. Draw and color pictures of the main characters on template #2.

5. Cut out both wheels. On template #2, cut out the section indicated.

6. Place the template #2 wheel on the wheel from template #1. Attach the center of the two wheels with a brad.

7. Write your name on the back of the story wheel.

8. Write the book title, author's name, and your name on the Story Wheel Activity Sheet.

9. Write a description of the three events on the activity sheet.

Story Wheel Template #1

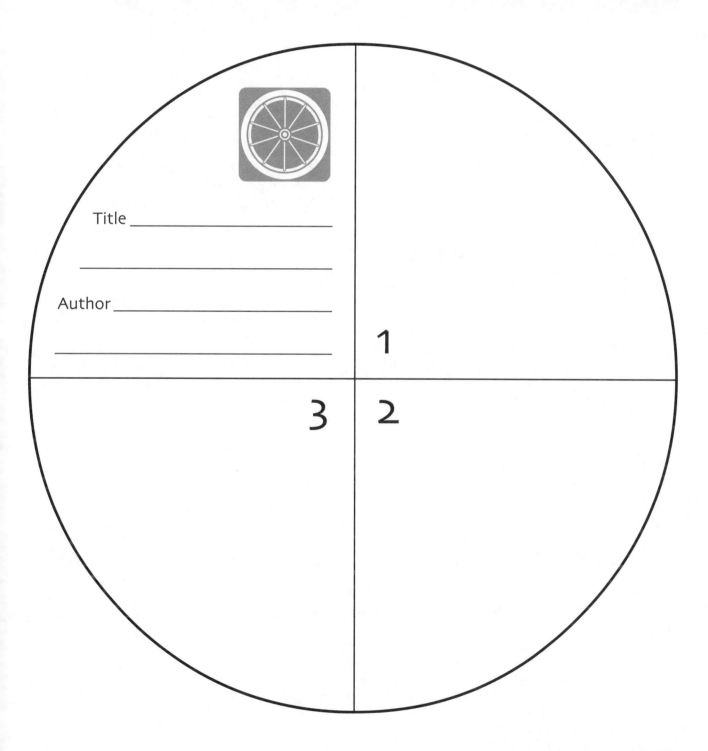

Title _____

_____

Author _____

_____

1

3 2

Story Wheel Template #2

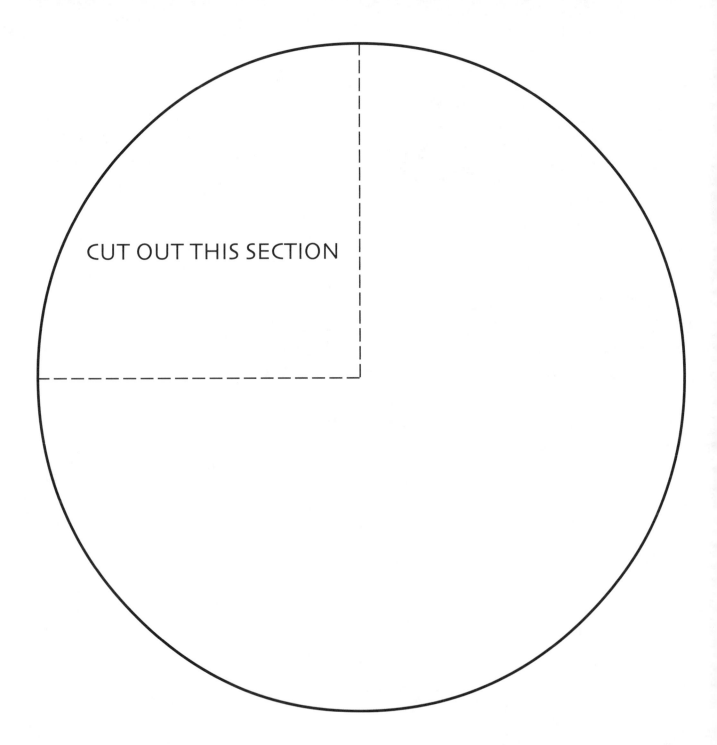

CUT OUT THIS SECTION

Story Wheel Activity Sheet

Name _____

Title _____

Author _____

Section 1 – Beginning _____

_____

_____

_____

Section 2 – Middle _____

_____

_____

_____

Section 3 – End _____

_____

_____

_____

_____

Accordion Story Map

What You Do:

1. Make a story map to plot the events from a book your group has read.

2. Write the book title and author's name on the Accordion Story Map Template. In the box, draw and color a picture of an important event in the book.

3. As a group, brainstorm which events should be included in the story map.

4. In the second section of the template, write about the events in the beginning and middle of the book.

5. In the last section, write about the events from the end of the book and your group's opinion of the book.

6. Cut out the story map. Fold the first section backwards on the dashed line. Fold the third section forward on the dashed line.

7. Turn the paper over so that the first section is showing. The story map should open like an accordion.

8. Write your name and the names of the classmates in your group on the back of the story map.

Note to the Teacher:
Assign students to small groups to read a book together.

What You need:
Accordion Story Map Template

pencil

colored pencils, markers, crayons

scissors

Accordion Story Map Template

Title _____

Author _____

Beginning

Middle

End

Our Opinion

Cloud Mobile

What You Do:

1. Create a cloud mobile of the events from a book you have read.

2. Label the sun on Cloud Mobile Template #1 with the book title and author's name. Write your name on the back.

3. Cut out the sun and punch a hole in the top. Tie a piece of yarn or string through the hole and hang the sun from a clothes hanger.

4. Gather four copies of template #2 and label the clouds as follows: Beginning, Middle, End, Opinion.

5. On each cloud, use complete sentences to describe the main events from the beginning, middle, and end of the book.

6. Write your opinion of the book on the fourth cloud.

7. Cut out all of the clouds. Then, punch a hole in the top and bottom of the first three clouds and tie pieces of yarn or string through the holes.

8. Punch a hole in the bottom of the sun and hang the clouds in order under it.

9. Punch a hole in the top of the Opinion cloud and tie it under the End cloud.

Note to the Teacher:
Make enough copies of Cloud Mobile Template #2 so that each student has four clouds.

What You Need:
Cloud Mobile Templates

pencil

scissors

hole punch

yarn or string

clothes hanger

Cloud Mobile Template #1

Title _____

_____

_____

Author _____

_____

Cloud Mobile Template #2

Flash Cards

What You Do:

1. Quiz yourself and your classmates with flash cards about a book your group has read.

2. As a group, brainstorm the questions you could ask about the characters, setting, and plot of the book.

3. Write a question about one of the characters on Flash Cards Template #1.

4. Write the answer to the question, book title, author's name, your name, and the names of the classmates in your group on the right side of the flash card.

5. Cut out the flash card.

6. Fold the card on the dashed line.

7. Glue or tape the two sides together to form the flash card.

8. Repeat these steps to complete the rest of the flash cards.

Notes to the Teacher:

- Assign students to small groups to read a book together.

- Make enough copies of the templates so that the groups can complete flash cards for each chapter or section of the book.

- If desired, you can combine the flash cards of all the groups for the class to play trivia games. You could also create a board game with the flash cards.

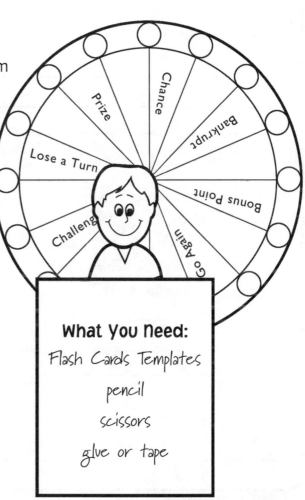

What You Need:
Flash Cards Templates
pencil
scissors
glue or tape

Flash Cards Template #1

CHARACTERS

_____

_____

_____

Answer _____

_____

_____

Title _____

_____

Author _____

Names _____

_____

SETTING

_____

_____

_____

Answer _____

_____

_____

Title _____

_____

Author _____

Names _____

_____

Flash Cards Template #2

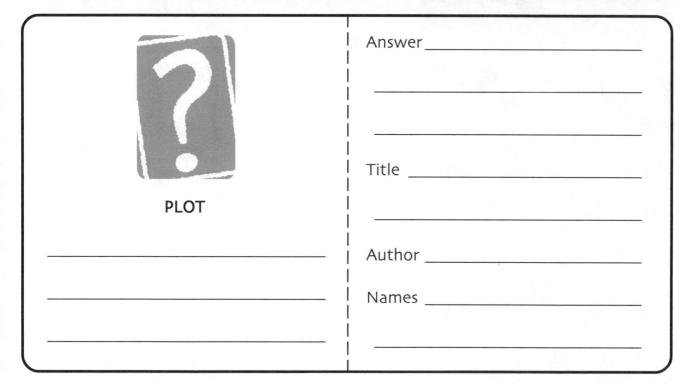

PLOT

_____

_____

_____

Answer _____

_____

_____

Title _____

_____

Author _____

Names _____

_____

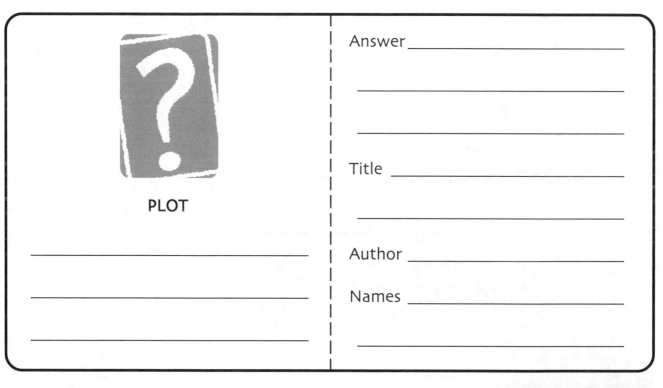

PLOT

_____

_____

_____

Answer _____

_____

_____

Title _____

_____

Author _____

Names _____

_____

Charm Bracelet

What You Do:

1. Make a charm bracelet of the important items from a book you have read.

2. List six important objects on the Charm Bracelet Template. For example, the basket, cookies, ax, and cape were some of the important objects in *Little Red Riding Hood*.

3. Draw and color a picture of each item on the charms on the template.

4. Cut out each charm and punch a hole in the top.

5. Braid three pieces of yarn to form a bracelet.

6. Loop a piece of yarn through the hole in each charm. Tie the ends of the yarn to the bracelet. Then, tie the charm bracelet around your wrist.

7. Write the book title, author's name, and your name on the template. Then, write why each object is important.

Notes to the Teacher:
- If desired, you can precut lengths of yarn.

- The length of the yarn for the bracelets should be longer so that the bracelets can be tied on the students' wrists. The lengths for the charms should be shorter.

- You could also attach the charms with twist ties or rubber bands. Twist ties can be purchased in a roll and cut to any length.

hole punch

scissors

yarn

What You Need:

colored pencils

Charm Bracelet Template

pencil

Charm Bracelet Template

Name _____

Title _____

Author _____

Charm   This charm is important because . . .

_____   _____

_____   _____

_____   _____

_____   _____

_____   _____

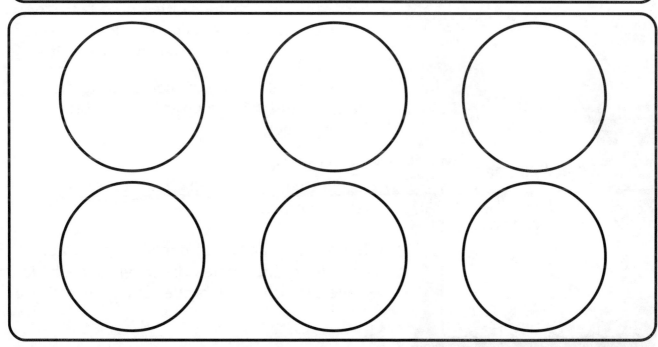

FAIRY TALE FUN

What You Do:

1. Compare and contrast two fairy tales your group has read by completing a Venn diagram.

2. Read the stories together, paying close attention to anything that is similar between them. For example, they both might have a stepmother or queen; they both might have characters in groups of three (three little pigs, three billy goats). Look for elements from the stories that are different, too.

3. Write the titles of the fairy tales above the circles on the Fairy Tale Fun Activity Sheet.

4. Compare the fairy tales on the Venn diagram. Write the similar items in the middle of the diagram where the circles overlap.

5. Write the ideas that are different in each story in the outside part of each circle. Be sure to write the information under the correct title.

6. Write your name and the names of the classmates in your group at the top of the activity sheet.

Notes to the Teacher:

- Assign students to small groups to read fairy tales together.

- This activity can also be done with the whole class. If this is a whole-class activity, you could make a transparency of the activity sheet.

What You Need:

Fairy Tale Fun Activity Sheet

pencil

Fairy Tale Fun Activity Sheet

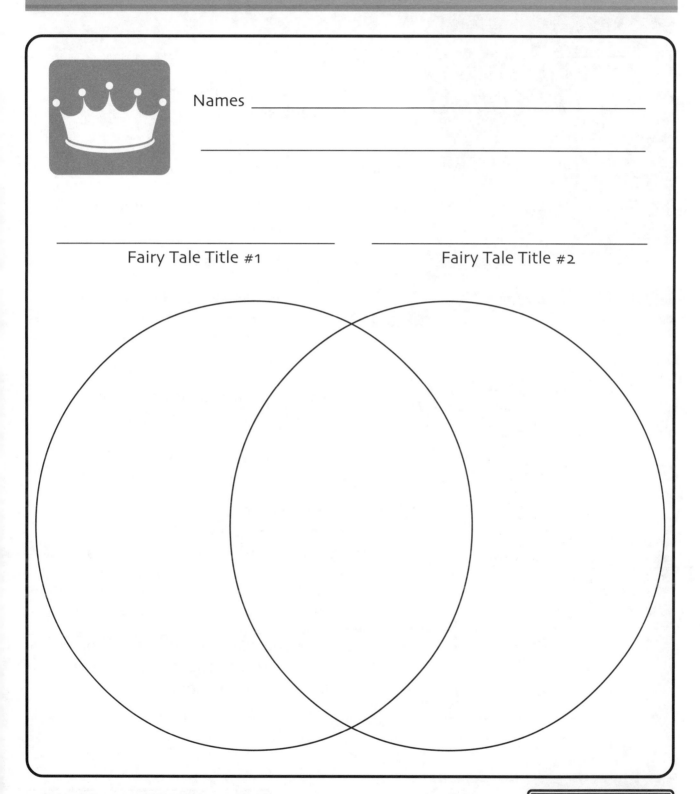

Names _____

_____

_____   _____
Fairy Tale Title #1   Fairy Tale Title #2

Favorite Books

What You Do:

1. Complete a favorite book card for a book you have read and enjoyed.

2. Write the book title and author's name on one of the cards on the Favorite Books Template.

3. In the next section, explain why you liked the book. Write in complete sentences.

4. Cut out the card.

5. On the back of the card, write the names of the main characters and describe the main events from the book.

6. Punch a hole in each circle at the top of the card and add it to two book rings.

7. Repeat these steps to make a favorite book card for another book you enjoy.

Notes to the Teacher:

- If desired, photocopy the Favorite Books Template on card stock for extra durability.

- Book cards can be displayed by hanging them on a bulletin board for students to read.

- If desired, you can make additional copies of the template so students can add to their favorite books throughout the year.

What You Need:

Favorite Books Template

pencil

scissors

hole punch

2 looseleaf book rings

Favorite Books Template

My Favorite Books

Title _____

Author _____

I like this book because . . .

_____

_____

_____

_____

My Favorite Books

Title _____

Author _____

I like this book because . . .

_____

_____

_____

_____

BOOK BLIZZARD BIBLIOGRAPHY

What You Do:

1. Create a book snowstorm by making a bibliography of books you have read.

2. Write the genre or topic of your bibliography on Book Blizzard Template #1. You could choose fairy tales, biographies, animals, sports, etc. All of the books you choose for your bibliography should be from the same genre or topic area.

3. Cut out the cloud and write your name on the back.

4. Tape the cloud to a clothes hanger.

5. Write the book title and the author's name on template #2. Then, write a summary of the book.

6. Cut out the snowflake. Draw and color a picture on the back to go with the summary.

7. Punch a hole in the top of the snowflake.

8. Tie a piece of yarn through the hole and tie the snowflake to the hanger.

9. Repeat steps 5–8 and add snowflakes for other books that fit with the genre or topic of your bibliography.

Notes to the Teacher:
- Make enough copies of template #2 so that students can make their bibliographies.

- Cut the yarn pieces to various lengths so that the snowflakes hang unevenly.

What You need:
Book Blizzard Templates
pencil
scissors
tape
clothes hanger
colored pencils, crayons
hole punch
yarn

Book Blizzard Template #1

Genre or Topic _____

Book Blizzard Template #2

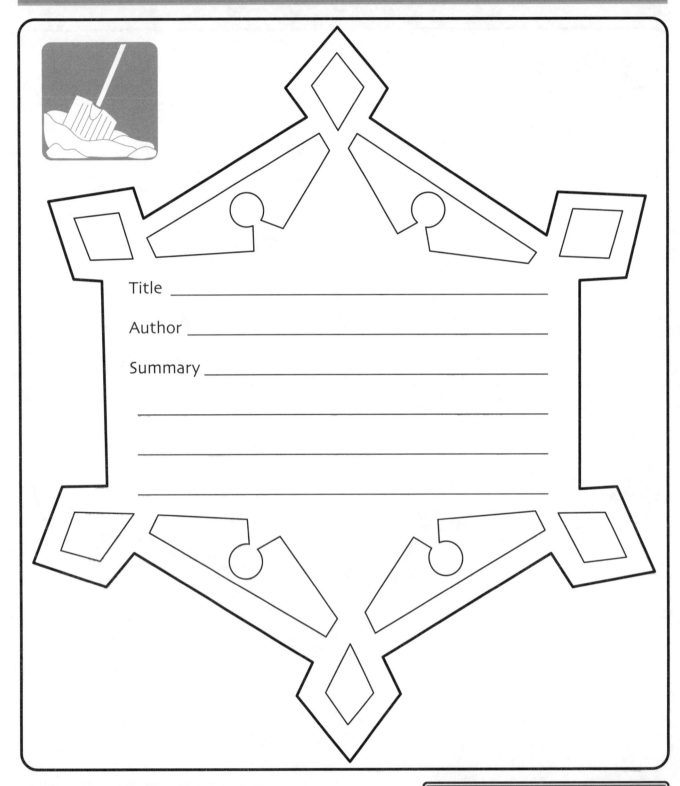

Title _____

Author _____

Summary _____

_____

_____

_____